prayers that saved my life

DR. CHERYL DIXON COLBURN

Prayers That Saved My Life
Copyright © 2014 by Cheryl Dixon Colburn
All rights reserved. No part of this book may be reproduced
or transmitted in any form or by any means without written
permission of the author.

All Scripture quotations are taken from the Amplifed Bible
version of the Holy Bible (paraphrased by author.)

ISBN-13: 978-0-9968715-0-1
ebook ISBN: 978-0-9968715-2-5

Printed in the United States of America

RevMedia Publishing
PO BOX 5172
Kingwood, TX 77325

A publishing division of Revelation Ministries
www.revmediapublishing.com

No part of this book may be reproduced or transmitted in any form
or by any means, electronic or mechanical—including photocopying,
recording, or by any information storage and retrieval system—
without permission in writing from the publisher.
Inquiries to permissionseditor@revmediapublishing.com.

1 2 3 4 5 6 7 8 9 10 11 21 20 19 18 17 16 15 14

Acknowledgments

"What a awesome & extraordinary job that Cheryl has done with this book of prayer! Each of these prayers are scriptural & are proven in communing with God!

"Her compilation of each prayer & presentation of each line shows a deep insight & emotion of love & passion for our Heavenly Father & our Lord Jesus Christ! You will grow in your communication with God as you say, read & memorize these prayers. Also the knowledge of God's word & promises will increase in your life. I highly recommend this book for prayer & meditation! Great job, Dr. Cheryl Dixon, for allowing the Holy Spirit to direct you in this project! Gods best to all who read & use this ministry tool!"

BLESSINGS,

Dr. Roger F. Siratt, D.D. / Th.M.
Director of Miracle Ministry Intn'l
Sr. Pastor of T.C.C. Family Church
Owner Mid-South Boys Musical Group

"Wouldn't it be wonderful to live a life without challenges, trials, problems or difficulties? Yet, as we go through life, we know that we are not immune from any of these obstacles. The question arises, "What do I do when facing these trying times?" In this book you will find how Cheryl took the Word of God and crafted prayers that she confessed, declared boldly and applied in her life.

"During times of physical, emotional and spiritual pain, I can recall Cheryl proclaiming these prayers as she walked through the church sanctuary and our home. She was resolute and determined not to wavier in any area of her life until total freedom and victory came, as she stood immovable on the eternal Word of God.

Hundreds and thousands of people just like yourself have read this book and are now experiencing the wonder working power of God in their lives. If you need a breakthrough and change in your life, I know this book will be a great blessing and help to you.

"Thank you, Cheryl, my amazing wife, for your unwavering faithfulness, committed purpose and dedication to the Lord, your family, church family and to me."

Dr. Gary Dixon, D.D.,S.Th.
Pastor/Founder Abundant Life Outreach Center

"I have known, and been a personal friend of, Reverend Doctor Cheryl Dixon for a long time! In all that time she has been a solid Word speaking, Word believing, Word praying woman of God. As a Christian counselor I have personally used this book, and given it to clients to build them up, push them on, and get them through the rough spots. It is simple, easy to read, easy to understand, and Scripture based only. The Word says "the fervent, EFFECTUAL prayer of a righteous man/woman avails MUCH!" The many promises spoken by inspiration of the Holy Spirit are ours to enjoy, and receive; however, if you don't know what they are-you can't appropriate what belongs to you, right? GET THIS BOOK and use it; it's concise, and you will benefit from what has taken Dr. Dixon years of personal time with the Holy Spirit and learning what God's grace and love has provided!"

Reverend Marilyn J. Fisher, Ph.D.
New Beginnings Christian Counseling

"Life Saving Prayers" by Dr. Cheryl Dixon has proven invaluable in my own self-growth and Christ driven mission.

"Pastor Dixon's heart charged prayers explode with popping

supernatural evidence of Christ Jesus Our Lord's personal presence! Each prayer touches how God has uniquely woven his sovereignty in all earthy relationships!"

    Sandra VanBoxel CSW (Certified Social Worker)
    CSW (Clinical Substance Abuse Counselor)
    ICS (Independent Clinical Supervisor)

"Are you desperate for God to answer your prayers? Do you need a miracle, a breakthrough that only the very Word of God Himself can bring? Then I recommend this prayer book that you can follow, believe, stand upon and speak out over yourself, circumstances and those that you love. You will be abundantly blessed and experience the understanding of the power and authority over the enemy (Satan and the kingdom of darkness) As I have. Your prayers and your words will be filled with God's words of life, truth and love which always defeats Satan."

    Mary Beth Neubauer – Intercessor
    Aglow International Ministries/
    President, MaryBeth Neubauer
    Lakeland Aglow Chapter, Minocqua, WI.

"Cheryl has dedicated her entire life to being a faithful servant to Jesus Christ, her Lord and Savior. In doing so, she has sought to hear God's voice in all of life's approaches, which has expanded her opportunities to minister to many people in the kingdom of God.

"Throughout the years she has developed a personal prayer life that has motivated her to put these prayers in a book for others to read and identify with in many conflicts and joys we experience in this life.

"I trust you will hear her heart of love and compassion that expresses

her consecration and dedication to the Lord. Each prayer must be understood in the expressive way which she has penned them to be ours too just as the psalms of David are to be applied to us today.

"Cheryl has spent many hours in training and education to be the instrument of God to teach and lead others into a victorious life. She is a woman of many talents and gifts. She is able to lead a praise team from the piano, and preach the word of God from the pulpit with a passion and devotion that only comes from the anointing of God.

"Therefore I can highly recommend this book of prayers to you without hesitation or trepidation, because I can personally attest to her personal relationship with the Lord and throughout the years she has never wavered, so allow this book to guide you and bless you in your spiritual journey."

Pastor Dester Cummins
Cheryl Dixon's Father

Foreword

It is an honor for me to recommend my good friend Dr. Cheryl Dixon's first book. When I first read "Declarations and Prayers" I was so moved that I carry this book with me everywhere I go. I encouraged her to get this book into as many hands as possible because prayer gets results. When you declare who you are in agreement with God's Word you can have confidence that He hears you and will bring desired answers and move mountains.

Cheryl is very specific and Biblical in her prayers and declarations because they come out of spending much intimate time with her Heavenly Father. This book is her personal spiritual journey that has resulted in her rock solid foundation of faith. This book will teach you how to form your own prayers. I personally have had spiritual enrichments in my prayer life as I use her book.

My family and I have personally heard angels worship with us as Cheryl led the praise team at Abundant Life Church where she and her husband Gary pastor. Our family is blessed to call them our cherished friends. Cheryl has proven God is faithful in every area of life. Pray these prayers, declare these declarations and your life will be changed.

King Jesus Is Coming Soon,
Dr. Gary Wood
Author of "A Place Called Heaven"

INTRODUCTION

I am deeply thankful to all those who have encouraged me along the way to put my personal prayers and declarations in writing and to share them with others.

These prayers are very personal to me, and in the beginning, were only meant for my eyes and God's ears. But, something happened along the way and others took note of things I would say or pray, so I felt led to put them in writing and make these available to others.

These prayers and declarations were written in some of the most trying and desperate times of my life, when circumstances came crushing down on me and fear was paralyzing. At times the stress was so great, it caused a bleeding ulcer that caused me much pain. Nights were long and sleeplessness would hit me as my mind came under attack.

I had to learn the Word on my own, no one could do it for me. No one else could renew my mind. I needed to take action myself. Faith without works is dead. You don't have to do anything to get saved and receive Jesus Christ into your heart, it's a free gift to all who will receive and ask Jesus into their lives. But, if you want to grow and live a victorious life in the here and now, you have get the Word in your heart yourself and that takes work.

Sometimes in the night I would get up and cry out to God for His help. I would look up Scriptures from God's Word, write them down in a journal, then formulate a prayer knowing God honors His Word above everything else. I would stay until I sensed Him touch me. I would find peace then go back to bed. God's Word has never failed me.

I would see answers to my prayers. No, they didn't come all at once. Sometimes answers came quickly and other times they seemed slow in coming, sometimes days, weeks, months or even years. But, I found God to be faithful to His Word every time. In these times of great trial and struggle, my faith grew the most. I developed a fellowship relationship with the Lord that developed into a deeper love than anything I have ever known. I heard it said there can be no testimony without a test. I believe that is true.

There was a time my husband, the love of my life, was given a death sentence from the doctor: stage level 4 cancer. The doctor said our lives would never be the same again.

We sat in disbelief as the doctor spoke. My husband and I didn't say a word until the doctor had finished speaking, then the doctor left the room to prepare for immediate surgery. A cloud of death entered the room and a dark heaviness wanted to overshadow us, yet the Word of God in our hearts came up in our spirit.

Right there in the doctor's office, we looked at each other and began declaring God's Word. "I will live and not die and declare the works of God. I am healed by the stripes of Jesus." He came to heal all sickness and disease. It was like bursts of light were being sent into the darkness as we spoke out living truth from God's Word. We were entering a battle, but chose to speak life. Now was the time we had to practice what we preached to our congregation all these years.

When fear would grip my heart, with the thought that I could lose this great man God had given me whom I love dearly, I would run to the Word and sometimes speak it out loud, so my own ears could hear it until I felt peace. I would speak God's Word until a supernatural calm would come over me. It was a fight to stay in faith because fear would try to control me. I had to get my emotions under control. I knew I could not be in faith and fear at the same time. So, I would pray and declare God's promises until the darkness was pushed back, until I felt peace, then I could pray in faith. I had to do this process many times until I had finally overcome, as it would try to come back again and again. Finally, the enemy could see I was not giving up, and victory was mine and he was defeated.

But, I found God's Word more powerful than anything else. I would take communion, pray in the Holy Ghost and declare the promises of God. I chose to get in agreement with what God had said. He is a higher authority, His Word is more real than what I can see, hear, taste, feel and touch. I refused to speak out any words of doubt and unbelief from my mouth and give the enemy anything to use against me.

My dear husband went into surgery and came out with a report that said: "We could not find any cancer." Praise the Lord. Jesus came to heal all sickness and disease. Never give up no matter what it looks like. God is more powerful than anything, even cancer. He has the Name above all names.

God had given us a vision for Eagle River and northern Wisconsin when we were in Bible school. He said our ministry would begin there. We moved to Eagle River and started a new church. Things were going well the first couple of years. We were seeing people get saved and the church was moving forward slowly as we earned the love and trust of the people and of our community.

A few years into it, some people rose up against us and wanted our church. The lies and accusations grieved me personally, so deeply. The words this one man spoke over me tore me up so badly and wounded me severely, causing my body to shake and it sent me into a darkness and despair that only the Lord could bring me out of. Those words were from Satan to try to destroy me and the call of God on my life.

For two years I didn't want to leave the house for fear I would run into this man. Without the Lord's intervention, I would have left the ministry and the call of God on my life and it would have affected my husband as well. I had to continue to pray and renew my mind and declare God's Word over my life and the circumstances. Was it easy? No, it was hard, yet in these years I grew so much in the Lord. It brought me strength and healing, and He renewed my spirit. Today, I am totally healed and restored.

Several years ago, a Christian couple introduced us to a financial investment. We were excited about it and got involved, but financial ruin was lurking at our door. Sometime later we found ourselves about to lose everything. This was a test that left us feeling defeated and embarrassed; we were pastors of a great church and it looked like we could not manage our own finances. Who would ever respect us or listen to us again? How could we ever be effective?

Again the sleepless nights would come with tears and fear of losing our church because of a stupid decision we made. So, again I would be up praying and writing Scriptures and speaking them out loud to drown out the voice of the enemy that was saying we would lose the precious church God gave us to pastor, and the precious people God had put in our lives to lead and teach them the Word of God, and our home and everything.

Over a two-year period, we told no one the battle we were fighting to save our home. We were so ashamed. One day we said, "It's over, we just can't do this anymore." I was so sick, my stomach hurt so bad with the bleeding ulcer acting up again. It was time to tell our church board. At this point I just wanted everyone to know. I was tired of carrying this alone. I just wanted to be free. Yet, God heard my prayers and the times I would cry out to Him for His help. He was there for us. He had a plan. He was not done with us yet!

As we were getting ready for a board meeting, we were prepared to resign the church with much shame and regret. Oh, how we loved these people. Our hearts were breaking. We didn't know what we were going to do or where we would go. We felt we had failed and we felt we were defeated; it was over. The precious vision that God so supernaturally gave us, it was done. This is just the way we felt.

As we entered the board meeting and told the board the battle we had been in for the last two years, before we could even get the words out of our mouths, one of the board members stepped up and said, "DON'T EVEN THINK ABOUT RESIGNING. You were there when my son needed you." And "You were there when my dad died." God was doing an amazing work.

Oh, how our hearts saw the glory of the Lord that day. They didn't care, they loved us and wanted us to stay. We had been through a great battle, but God turned everything around for us in a short time, because of His Word. As praying people, we saw God bring the right people at the right time when needed. It does not always turn out like we think, but God knows exactly what to do and how to do it. We must trust Him. Praise the Lord.

After 27 years as pastors of Abundant Life Church, we saw God moving and things were happening, services were good, the church was growing, people's lives were being touched and changed. We were overflowing with people and we really needed more room. My husband and I had been talking about an addition to the church and the people knew we needed more room. But, my husband was determined not to make a move unless God said it was time. My husband, Gary, believed when God said it's time, He would pay for it. We don't want any mortgage on God's house.

A strong anointing came upon me one morning and God spoke to my heart to tell the people that when $100,000 is raised, we are to start the new addition. With the approval of my husband, I stood before the people and told them what the Lord had said.

At that very moment, several people stood up. One said, "I will give $1000." Another said, "I will give $1000" and another $2000 and a few more. Something new started that day. In a difficult economy, the money was raised in only four to five months and we began the building. The first $100,000 was just the start, then we paid as we went. We saw supernatural increase take place. We were able to buy the land next to the church for parking. We had prayed for the land for over 15 years and the day came when we did buy it. God honors His Word.

I can go on and on of how God built this building. When we needed it, it came! It was God's time, not ours. It's been two years and we have paid cash and we have no mortgage. As of this writing, the building is almost totally complete and paid for. The favor Scriptures really work! God's Word works.

One day my husband was working late at the office at church and he heard something outside in the back of the building. As he went to investigate, he found a boy trying to light the new addition on fire. What a close call! But, God protected His house. He is alive and powerful.

There are so many stories I could share of the power of

prayer, like a man being raised from the dead, our son being protected from a potentially fatal accident, to the deaf hearing, the blind seeing, and the lame walking. What God will do for one, He will and can do for you.

Remember if your faith level is low, that means your Word level is low. Faith comes by hearing and hearing the Word of God. That includes you speaking it out of your mouth. Blessings and cursing cannot come from the same mouth. What you say is revealing what you believe. Speaking God's Word and making it first place will change your thinking to think like God. When we get in agreement with Him and say what He says over our lives, that is when we see our prayers answered.

For me, personally, I wanted to learn God's heart, His will and how to pray effectively. I found out that God honors His Word above everything else. He's not moved by our moaning and groaning. He is moved by the power of His Word. So, I began to say what God says in His Word over my life, circumstances and for those that I would pray for.

As time went on, I began to understand what it meant by "the washing of the water of the Word" over my life. Somehow, I felt so refreshingly empowered and I began to see results. I made a commitment to line up my words with His supernatural Words. I got in agreement with what He said about me and my circumstances. I have never been the same since. The Word of God has changed my life. I have learned living His Word is more than just speaking it over my life once in a while, but making it a life style. As His daughter, every day I declare the goodness of God and His promises to me.

Truly, there is something about hiding His Word in your heart; for out of it flows the issues of life.

As you read through this book, I pray that the truth of God's Word will come alive and be revealed to you as it has for me.

I am so grateful for all those who have sown into my life and inspired me through their walk with God by their example, writings and teachings.

My husband, Dr. Gary Dixon - He is the love of my life. His support and encouragement to me has never wavered. He is the greatest man I have even known. A man of honor, integrity and strength. Where I have been weak, he has been my strength I will always love you!

Dr. Gary Wood - who encouraged me so much. Dr. Jerry Savelle (His Book *"Walking In Divine Favor"*) taught me how to walk in the favor of God. Mike Murdock, Cheryl Prewitt Salem, Jentezen Franklin and Bob Buess (His book *"Favor The Road To Success"*).

Special thanks to my parents, Rev. Dester Jay and Barbara Cummins, who kept us kids in church and raised us to know the Lord. Their love and support has been such an encouragement.

Table of Contents

PERSONAL DECLARATION 19

ENCOURAGMENT 21

PERSONAL CONFESSION OF FAITH 25

CONFIDENCE 27

GUIDANCE 29

GOD'S PURPOSE FOR MY LIFE 31

HEALING 33

BEING A SUCCESS 35

FAVOR I 37

FAVOR II 39

PRAYER FOR THE CHURCH 41

BLESSING 43

PRAYER FOR CALLING IN YOUR HARVEST 47

POSSESSING YOUR PROMISE - FINANCES 49

PROTECTION 51

FULFILLING MY ASSIGNMENT 53

PRAY THE WORD - Psalm 119 57

FAMILY 59

MY JABEZ PRAYER - 1 Chronicles 4:10 61

PERSONAL DECLARATION

In this year, I will experience greater victories and answered prayer more than ever before. Doors will be opened to me that have not opened before. I will go beyond the limitations that have been there in the past, and I will break through walls and barriers that I've never been able to break through before. I am living in the last days' and God's favor greatly abounds on my life as never before. I receive all that belongs to me. I expect freedom and victory in every area. I expect restoration and increase. Money comes to me.

I walk in God's unmerited favor. I walk in the exceeding riches of His grace. I will experience the tangible things I can see; the above and beyond. My cup runs over. I have every kind of favor, more than anything I have ever experienced before.

Because I am in Christ Jesus and I live upright before Him, I will experience the immeasurable, limitless, surpassing riches of His free grace, His unmerited favor in kindness, and goodness of heart toward me in Christ Jesus. (Eph. 2:7)

The set time of grace and favor is upon my life. The Lord shows up to support, endorse, assist, make easier, feature, provide me with advantages, and grant me special privileges.

As the Prophets have spoken, so be it unto me.

Thank You, Jesus, for answered prayer. I give You all the Glory and Honor due Your holy name.

I love You! Amen.

ENCOURAGMENT

All nations call me blessed for I shall be a delightsome land. I am the righteousness in God. I, in righteousness, shall be established. Because God lives in me, I cannot fail. I am loved with an everlasting love.

I now seek first the Kingdom of God and His righteousness and all things shall be added unto me. I shall be taught of the Lord and great shall be my peace and undisturbed composure.

I am precious and valuable to God and He has made unto me wisdom, righteousness, sanctification and redemption through His blood.

I shall not criticize, judge or condemn. I am born to win. I love myself, so I can effectively love others.

No weapon formed against me or my family shall prosper. I am the target of my Father's love. The apple of His eye. God is my exceedingly great reward.

God will supply all my needs according to His riches in Glory through Christ Jesus. He meets the desires of my heart. He withholds no good thing from me. Whatsoever state that I am in, I have learned to be content.

I can do all things through Christ which strengthens me. God has not given me a spirit of fear, but of power, of love and of a sound mind. I cast down, put to death, all thoughts and imaginations that are not pleasing to You, Father. I refuse to dwell on them in Jesus' name.

I am the head and not the tail. I am above and not beneath. I am the favored one of God and man favors me also. I have been crowned with glory and honor.

I am blessed going in and blessed going out. I am blessed in the city and blessed in the field. I am blessed in the fruit of my body. Increase is coming into my life and lots of it.

According to my Father, so be it unto me. I give no place to Satan. Greater is He that is in me than he that is in the world.

I speak under the anointing of the Holy Ghost and out of my mouth rolls the wisdom of God. I have an instructed tongue. I hear the voice of the Good Sheppard and the voice of a stranger I will not follow.

The anointing destroys the yoke. I am anointed. My husband and I flow together under the same anointing in the name of Jesus.

I have no eyes to see, no ears to hear, mouth to speak, feet to move except when directed by Jesus Christ, my Savior.

I will never give up; I will not fall or stumble. never give in to depression or discouragement. I overcome a low self esteem. I am a child of the King. I see myself as God sees me through the blood of Jesus.

PERSONAL CONFESSION OF FAITH

I am the Body of Christ. Satan has no power over me. I overcome evil with good. Greater is Jesus that lives in me than Satan that dwells in the world. I am far from oppression. Fear does not come near me. Thank You, God!

I am redeemed from the curse of the law. I am redeemed from poverty, sickness and spiritual death. It is true unto me according to the Word of God. I am the head and not the tail. Thank You, God, for making me the head. I am from above and not from beneath. I belong to God.

I am not ashamed of the gospel of Jesus. I am not ashamed of the healing of the Lord. I am not ashamed to speak with new tongues; therefore by faith, I declare these things; I am healthy, I am prosperous, and my soul is prospering in the knowledge of the Lord Jesus, even Jesus the Word. I cannot be conquered. I will not be defeated. For me to fail, God would have to fail, and God cannot fail.

This is what I have. This is who I am. I am washed in the blood of Jesus and I am a child of the King! My God is the God of Joy and I am His child; therefore, I am a joy maker. I am a lot of fun to be around. In the presence of the Lord is fullness of joy; therefore, the world cannot take it away.

(Originally by Dr. Roger Siratt. Used by permission.)

I belong to God and I am a blast to be around. My God is the God of Peace. I am His child; therefore, I am a peacemaker. It is hard to make me mad. Oh! I am just like the Lord. I am slow to wrath and I am of great mercy. My God is the God of Love and I am His child; therefore, I am just a big old love bomb spreading God's love and sharing His love by telling others of Jesus.

Amen. So be it unto me and unto the Body of Christ.

CONFIDENCE

I have been crowned with Glory and Honor. (Ps. 8:3-5) I abide and serve You, Lord, and I bear fruit so my Father will be honored. (John 12:26) Thank You, Lord, for making Your face to shine upon me and my family today. You are so gracious to me. You lift up Your countenance upon me and give me peace. (Num. 6:25-26) If You are for me, who can be against me? You spared not Your own Son's life, but delivered Jesus up for all of us. How shall You, Lord, not freely give us all things? (Rom. 8:31-32)

Grace and favor are with me because I love my Lord, Jesus Christ, in sincerity. (Eph. 6:24) Jesus increased in wisdom and stature and in favor with God and man. Thank You, Lord, that I am increasing in wisdom and stature and in favor with You and man. (Luke 2:25)

Thank You, Lord, for giving me power when I faint and become weary. To those who have no might You increase strength, causing it to multiply and making it to abound. (Is. 40:29)

I wait for You, Lord. I expect, look for, and hope in You. You shall renew my strength and power. I lift up my wings and mount up close to God as eagles mount to the sun. I shall run and not be weary. I shall walk and not faint or become tired. (Is. 40:31)

I will not fear for You are with me. I do not look around in terror or dismay for You are my God. You said You would strengthen and harden me to difficulties. Yes, You will help me. You will hold me up and retain me with Your victorious right hand of righteous justice. (Acts 18:10) (Is. 41:10)

I expect a supernatural encounter.

I shall not be put to shame because I wait for, look and hope for, and expect You, Lord. (Is. 49:23) I have set You, Lord, continually before me. Because You are at my right hand, I shall not be moved. My heart is glad and my glory (inner self) rejoices. My body shall rest and confidently dwell in safety. (Ps. 16:8-9)

You will show me the path of life. In Your presence is fullness of joy. At Your right hand there are pleasures forevermore. (Ps. 17:11) You are good unto those that wait for You; to the soul that seeks You. (Lam. 3:25)

Because I have faith even as a grain of mustard seed, nothing is impossible for me. (Matt 17:20) You are with me and You keep me in all places, wherever I go. (Gen. 28:15)

GUIDANCE

Dear Jesus,

Guide me in Your truth and faithfulness. Teach me, O Lord, for You are the God of my salvation. On You I wait all day long. (Ps. 25:5)

You lead the humble in what is right and You teach me Your way. (Ps. 25:9)

Because I worship (fear) You, Lord, You will lead me in the way I should choose. I dwell at ease and my offspring will inherit the land. (Ps. 25:12-13)

Your secrets You show to those who worship, fear and revere You. You reveal their deep inner meaning to me. (Ps. 25:14)

You are my God forever and ever. You will be my guide even until death. (Ps. 48:14) Guide me with Your counsel and afterward receive me to glory and honor. (Ps. 73:24)

Thank You, Lord, for guiding me continually and satisfying me in drought and in dry places. You make my bones strong and I shall be like a watered garden and like a spring whose waters never fail. (Is. 58:11)

Thank You, Lord, for the Spirit of Truth for He will guide me into all truth. He will tell me Your heart and tell me things to come concerning the future. (John 16:13)

I can know and understand the counsels and purposes of You, Lord, as to guide and instruct me. Because I have the mind of Christ, I hold the thoughts, feelings and purposes of Your heart. (1 Cor. 2:16)

I will live and walk in the Holy Spirit, responsive to, controlled, and guided by Him, and then I will not gratify the cravings and desires of the flesh of human nature without God. (Gal. 5:16)

Teach me Your way, O Lord, and lead me in a plain path because of my enemies. (Ps. 27:11) Guide me with Your eyes. (Ps. 32:8) Because I am good in Your sight, You order my footsteps. (Ps. 37:23)

I commit my way unto You, Lord. I trust in You and You will bring it to pass. (Ps. 37:5) You lead me in paths I have not known. You will make darkness light before me and crooked things straight for me. (Is. 42:16)

Thank You, Jesus, with all my heart. Amen.

GOD'S PURPOSE FOR MY LIFE

Dear Jesus,

I cry unto You, my God, for You are performing on my behalf and rewarding me. Thank You, Lord, that You are bringing to pass Your purpose for my life; and what You started, You will complete. (Ps. 57:2)

After David fulfilled Your will and purpose for his life in his own generation, he then fell asleep in death. Thank You, Jesus, that I will also fulfill my life and destiny. The enemy will not cut it short, in the name of Jesus, for I will live long on the face of the earth because I obey and honor Your Word. (Acts 13:36)

I will not have to accomplish Your purpose in my life alone or in my own strength. For You, O Lord, are effectually at work in me, energizing and creating in me POWER and DESIRE to want to serve You for Your good pleasure, satisfaction and delight. Thank You, Jesus! You have made me adequate to accomplish my purpose and capable of fulfilling all the plans You have prepared and predestined ahead of time for me to walk in.

I have desire, Lord, that You placed in my heart and in my spirit - a desire that burns deep within and passions for You and Your presence; a passion that wants to please and serve. You gave me ability to accomplish this God-given desire. Continue, O Lord, to develop this ability to bring You honor and glory.

During times of preparation and training, work in me, teach me, and show me what I need to change to be able to move forward. Help me get over things in my life that would hold me back from moving on with You. Reveal to me things that would not please You and show me things that honor You. Prepare me for promotion.

Help me, Lord, to be a person of integrity, honor, and a person of my word. I will do what I say to carry out and fulfill my word, just as You do.

Show me how to finish what I start and give me the strength for this task. Thank You, Jesus, for planning for me and giving my life purpose.

HEALING

Father, in the name of Jesus, I thank You for sending Your Son to die for me and taking away all my sins. I thank You for taking those stripes on Your back for me to be whole. You came to heal all sickness and all disease. You gave Your life, so I could live. You came to heal and restore life to me today. I give You praise!

You came to bring me life and life more abundantly. The thief comes to steal, kill and destroy. You defeated the enemy and he has no power over me. There is the life-giving blood of Jesus Christ between us.

I declare this very day that I am healed by the stripes of Jesus and no weapon formed against me shall prosper. I will live and not die and declare the works of God.

Lord, You said that we would prosper in body, soul, and spirit as our minds prosper. So, I make a decision today that I am prospering my mind on the Word of God every day and my faith is growing. The Holy Spirit is quickening the living Word to me and health and healing are flowing into my body right now in Jesus' name.

I declare that I am healthy and whole from the top of my head to the soul of my feet. And I will continually give You thanks and praise for this wonderful miracle.

I will not be moved by how I feel or what it may look like. I am not denying that I am fighting a battle, but I am denying its right to stay in my body in the name of Jesus.

Thank You for my healing and for strengthening my spirit to stand as long as it takes. I am whole in Jesus' name. Amen.

BEING A SUCCESS

Father, I come before You in the name of Jesus.

I thank You for making me strong, wise, quick, sharp, bright, alert and fun to be around; that my life today will be a major blessing to those I come in contract.

I am rich (whole) and I never run out of money. I have sufficiency for all things and grace abounds towards me as I give ungrudgingly. I have great favor with people; they like me and I like them. They do nice things for me and they don't even know why. The desires of my heart come to pass. I am the favored one of God and man. His purpose is being fulfilled in me.

To be wealthy, healthy and whole is my right and privilege as a child of the Most High God. Jesus Christ did a complete work on the cross for me and I have been washed in His precious blood and cleansed from all unrighteousness. I am made new.

I am a success. I have favor. I am flowing in God's love today. People are blessed through my life and ministry. Today, I release God's miracle-working power. Others receive healing both in mind and body through my words and ministry because of the power of our Lord, Jesus Christ.

I am being filled and flooded with God's fullness. I am rooted and grounded in love. My Father is doing all that I ask and think. His power is taking over in me.

The Lord makes His face to shine upon me and He is gracious to me today. He loves me with an everlasting love. There is a river of favor flowing on my life because I walk upright before Him. I am not easily offended or hurt because I love His Word.

I expect miracles to unfold before me today in the name of Jesus Christ. Amen.

FAVOR I

(Ps. 5:11-12) Because we trust and take refuge in You, You put a covering over us and defend us. We love Your name. We will be joyful in You and be in high spirits because You bless the righteous with a shield and You surround us with goodwill, pleasure and favor.

(Ps. 37:3-5) I trust in You, Lord, lean, rely on and am confident in You. I do good, so I will dwell in the land and feed surely on Your faithfulness. Truly, my family and I are fed. I delight myself in You, Lord, and You give me the desires and secret petitions of my heart. I commit my ways to You. I roll each care of this load on You, Jesus. I trust in You and am confident You will bring it to pass.

(Prov. 14:9) Thank You, Jesus, that among the upright there is favor of God. (Prov. 22:1) Loving kindness and favor is better than silver and gold. (Prov. 30:5-7) Your anger is but for a moment, but Your favor is for a lifetime and Your favor is life.

Weeping may endure for a night, but joy comes in the morning. I will not be moved. By Your favor, You have established me as strong as a mountain.

(Is. 30:18) Jesus, I am so glad You earnestly wait, expecting, looking, and longing to be gracious to me and my family. You said You lifted Yourself up, so You may have mercy and show loving kindness to us today. You are a God of justice.

We are blessed, fortunate and to be envied because we earnestly wait for You - for Your victory, Your favor, Your love, Your peace, Your joy, and Your matchless unbroken companionship.

(Prov. 89:17) Lord, You are the glory of our strength, our proud adornment; and by Your favor, our horn (strength) is exalted and we walk with uplifted faces!

(Ps. 101:13) You are arising, Lord, on our behalf with mercy and loving kindness (favor). For it is time to have pity and compassion for us. Yes, the set time has come; the moment designated.

(Eph. 2:7) Thank You, Jesus, for all You have done. You clearly demonstrated through the ages Your immeasurable, limitless, unsurpassed riches of Your free grace, Your unmerited favor in Your kindness and goodness of heart toward us.

FAVOR II

I thank You Lord, for Your favor on my life. Your Word says You delight in me and my enemies cannot triumph over me. You uphold me in my integrity and righteousness. You set me in Your presence forever. (Psalms 41:11,22)

Your favor brings me honor in difficult times of trials, adversity and hardships. You cause things to turn around for me even though I can't see it in the natural. I believe it is happening now in Jesus' name. I overcome. (Exodus 11:3)

There are supernatural increase and promotions that come to me because of Your favor. Thank you, Jesus, for restoration of everything the enemy has stolen from me over the years. My life is being made complete and whole. (Genesis 39:21,23, Exodus 3:21)

Because Your favor is upon me, increased assets, land, money and provision are coming to me in Jesus' name. I experience the greatest blessings and victories in the midst of unfavorable odds. (Deuteronomy 33:23, Joshua 11:20)

Your favor is bringing to me recognition, prominence and preferential treatment; Your favor shows up to make things easier for me. I am the head and not the tail, from above and not beneath! (Esther 2:17, 1 Samuel 16:22)

At the right time and at the right place, ungodly civil authorities will issue policies, rules, regulations and laws to be changed or reversed to my advantage according to Your will. (ESTHER 8:5, 5:8)

You fight for me. Your favor and grace cause an ease in my life that You fight my battles because I walk upright before You. (PSALMS 44:3)

(Ps. 115:11-18) I respect You, Lord. I trust and lean only upon You for You are my help and shield. I'm so glad You're mindful of me. You bless me indeed. You know my needs and desires. You know right where I am at this time in my life, and You understand.

Thank You, dear Jesus, that blessings are on their way into our lives whether we are great or small in the eyes of man. You promised increase on us more and more and upon our children as well. Truly, we are blessed of the Lord. I will bless You affectionately and gratefully praise You, Lord, from this time forth and forever.

As of this day, I walk forward in the Favor of God. It rests richly upon me and my family. We live in the hour in which the Favor of God is being poured out upon the Church of Jesus Christ.

I have kept a Journal over the years. I try to write down when I have seen God's Favor. It does increase when you recognize it and acknowledge it. Be sure to give God the praise. It's so encouraging to your faith when you do this.

PRAYER FOR THE CHURCH

Father, I come to You in the mighty name of Jesus.

I pray over (your church) today and I ask You, Lord, to let it be a powerful healing station. May we never run out of money, may we have sufficiency for all things (Eph. 2:10) and may every need be met.

May we do the good works that You have planned for us to walk in; living the good life, which You prearranged and made ready for us to live.

Let the anointing be strong, the presence of the Holy Spirit be evident, and may many souls be saved, delivered and set free. We declare the Holy Spirit is being poured out, the prophetic is right on, bodies are healed, poverty is broken, the poor become rich, and the Devil's power is crushed in the mighty name of Jesus.

We thank You, Father, that properties, buildings, and land come to us in the name of Jesus. We reach out and reach many for the Kingdom of God. We take this land and build. It won't be long. It's happening now; debt- free in Jesus' name. Thank You for great favor as we go forward to accomplish the work You have set before us.

Bless our Pastors! Lead and guide them, strengthen them and grant unto them wisdom to fulfill the call.

May we always pray for them, support them, speak well of them and do our part.

Honorable people take places of leadership and support the vision. This body is productive for the Glory and Honor of God. Every person is blessed, needed and valuable.

Carry out Your purpose and do superabundantly far over and above all that we could dare ask or think; infinitely beyond our highest prayers, desires, thoughts, hopes and dreams.

To Him be Glory in the church in Jesus' name. Amen.

Thank You, Father, for hearing this prayer and answering your children. We give You all the praise and glory in Jesus' name, Amen.

BLESSING

Father,

I would like to thank You that I walk in "The Blessing" zone.

I am the head and not the tail. I am above only and not beneath. I am blessed in the city and blessed in the field. I am blessed coming in and blessed going out. I am blessed in my basket and kneading trough.

My enemies scatter seven ways. I am the favored one of God and man favors me also. I lend to many nations and do not borrow. People shall see I am called of the Lord and that I have been in His presence.

Jesus, You set me free from the curse of the law of sin and death. I live in the law of the Spirit of Christ Jesus. No good thing will You withhold from me because I walk uprightly before You.

I listen diligently to Your voice and I am watchful to do all Your commandments; then You set me on high above all the nations of the earth and all these blessings overtake me.

I hear the voice of the good Shepherd and the voice of a stranger I will not follow.

I seek You and Your Kingdom and Your righteousness first and all these things are added unto me.

It is Your desire that I prosper (materially) and be in health (physically) as my soul prospers (spiritually).

Blessed is the fruit of my body and the ground I walk upon. Every place I put my foot, You have given it to me. I am blessed in my storehouse and in everything I do.

You show up to endorse, help and assist me because I honor Your Word. You never leave me nor forsake me. You notice everything I do, every seed I plant, and every prayer I pray. You incline Your ear to my cry.

You're doing the miracles necessary to get us out of debt and keep us out of debt.

I receive the harvest of the hundred-fold return in this lifetime in Jesus' name.

Thank You, Jesus, for dying for my salvation, taking those stripes on Your back for my healing, and becoming poor that I might become rich.

I am the seed of Abraham and all these blessings overtake me because I am an heir of salvation and a joint heir with Christ.

I am a generous person and I shall be made fat! (complete, made whole, and enriched) (Prov. 11:25)

Thank You, Father, that "The Blessing" is on my life. I wear it like a coat and I notice and see the results all around me in Jesus' name. In due season, I will reap because I faint not.

You are the God of the superabundance. You are doing far over and above all that I could ever ask or think. You are going beyond my highest prayers, desires, thoughts, hopes and dreams. (Eph. 3:20)

I give You all the praise and glory for all that You are, all that You have done, and all that You are doing. Thank You, Father, in Jesus' name. Amen. (Deut. 28)

PRAYER FOR CALLING IN YOUR HARVEST

(James 5:4) As I'm serving You in the harvest field Lord, the wages that are due me will not be held back. They cry out to come to me, and my cry has reached the ears of the Lord of the Harvest. My harvest is coming unto me.

(Ps. 113:7-8) Thank You, Lord, that You have raised me out of the dust and You have lifted me out of the lowest shame and deepest poverty. You set me with princes.

(Prov. 13:22) Because I am a good man/woman, I leave an inheritance to my children's children. The wealth of the wicked has been laid up for me.

(Job 27:13-17) Even though the wicked heap up silver like dust and pile up clothing like clay, I will wear it, and because I am innocent I will divide the silver.

(Prov. 28:8) Because I give to the poor, I will receive the wealth of those who have gained increase through excessive interest and unjust efforts.

(Eccl. 2:26) God is giving me wisdom, knowledge and joy because I am good in His sight. But to the sinner, He gives the work of gathering and collecting, so that they may give to the righteous.

(Eccl.3:14) I know that whatever God does will endure forever. Nothing can be added or taken away from it. God does that so that we will worship Him; knowing that He is.

(Ps. 35:27) Let those who favor my righteous cause and have pleasure in my righteousness, shout for joy and be glad and say continually, "Let the Lord be magnified who takes pleasure in the prosperity of His children."

POSSESSING YOUR PROMISE-FINANCES

Dear Father, in the name of Jesus,

I thank You so much that You desire that I prosper and be in health even as my soul prospers. (3 John 2) I make a decision to prosper my soul and my mind on Your Word today and every day. I prosper in everything I set my hand to do and I receive Your promise, Lord, that I will walk in health to fulfill the plan and destiny You have for me. My life will not be cut short for I walk upright before You.

I will not let the Word of God depart from my mouth, but I will meditate on it day and night. I will do what it says, for then I will make my ways prosperous and I will deal wisely and have good success. (Joshua 1:8)

I rejoice in You today and I am glad that You are taking pleasure in prospering me. (Ps. 35:27) You are the One who gives the power to get wealth that Your covenant may be established. (Deut. 8:18)

In the name of Jesus, I arise today for Your light has come and Your glory (honor, splendor, power, wealth, authority, magnificence, fame, dignity, riches and excellency) has risen upon me. (Is. 60:1) I give You praise and glory that You are arising over me and Your glory is being seen upon me. (Is. 60:2) For You, O Lord, watch over the way of the righteous. (Ps. 1:6)

Your plans are good plans; plans to prosper me and not to harm me; plans to give me a hope and a great future. (Jer. 29:11)

I am like a tree planted by streams of water which yields its fruit in season and whose leaf does not wither. Whatever I do prospers. (Ps. 1:3) All who see me flourishing in prosperity will recognize and acknowledge that we are the people whom the Lord has blessed. (Is. 61:9) I pray that my life will be a testimony to the glory and honor of my Lord, Jesus Christ.

PROTECTION

Father, in the name of Jesus, I pray and confess Your Word over my life. I thank You that You watch over Your Word to perform it. I confess and believe that I am disciplined and taught of the Lord and obedient to Your will. Great is my peace and undisturbed composure. You give me safety and ease in every part of my life.

Father, You are perfecting all that which concerns me. I commit and cast the care of my load upon You once and for all. I know that I am in Your hands and I am persuaded that You are able to guard and keep that which I have committed to You. You are more than enough!

I choose life and love. Lord, I obey Your voice and cling to You for You are the life and length of my days. Therefore, I am the head and not the tail and shall be above only and not beneath.

Thank You for giving angels charge over me today to accompany, defend and preserve me in all my ways. You are my Lord, my Refuge and my Fortress. You are my Glory and the Lifter of my head.

The enemy is turned back from operating in my life in the name of Jesus. I go forward following Him with all my heart and soul. I increase in wisdom and in favor with God and man. I will resist temptation to do wrong.

Thank You, Jesus, that You will never leave me nor forsake me. You are always there to help me. I give You all the praise and the glory in Jesus' name. Thank You for honoring this prayer. Amen.

FULFILLING MY ASSIGNMENT

Dear Heavenly Father,

I come to You in the name of Jesus. Help me, Lord, to be willing and obedient to go where I have never been before and to create something I have never had before. Help me to leave my past behind that I may enter into the future You have planned for me to walk in. May I be certain about what you want for me. Help me to communicate it clearly to others when necessary.

Show me clearly the people to whom I have been assigned to help in fulfilling their assignments and dreams. In doing this, You bring the right people into my life to help me fulfill the things You have assigned me to do.

Even without encouragement from anyone, help me to be strong and have courage to do the things I know You have called me to do. Guide me in recognizing the people you are connecting me to. Guide me in being in the right place at the right time.

Help me to make wise decisions that move me in the right direction and persistent in following them out according to the leading of the Holy Spirit.

May I respect the mentorship and the experience of those older than I; those You bring into my life to help bring wisdom and guidance.

As I am honest and open about my needs, You will send those to care and help me as I am serious about my work. Productive people are responsive to me because I am productive. I know You can get anyone to me, anytime, wherever I am, to meet whatever need I have.

I am so thankful for everything You have done for me. Help me to notice even the small things in life and be appreciative. A grateful heart creates the atmosphere for You to move.

May I always try to be understanding and knowledgeable of the business of my husband. May I always respect and honor him and see the good in the man You gave me.

I will be accessible, agreeable, and aggressive in my assignment. I will not be lazy and allow discouragement to enter my heart. As You strengthen me, I will stay focused and keep my eyes on You and my assignment. I will walk with integrity, compassion, and purity in all my ways of obedience and service unto You.

I will protect the reputation of another, rather than destroying it. I will only speak well of others or I will not say anything; for I know that I will reap what I sow.

I know You will never look at my past and hold it against me as You move me into my future. My past is forgiven. Today is a new day - a new beginning!

Thank You, Jesus, for honoring this prayer and confession of faith. May I continue to become more and more like You. I love You. Amen.

PRAY THE WORD - Psalm 119

I am happy, fortunate, and to be envied because I keep Your Word in my heart. I do not wander from Your Word. I walk in Your ways. My ways are directed and established by hearing, receiving, loving and obeying Your Word.

I will never be put to shame or fail to inherit Your promises because I honor and respect Your Word. My thoughts and conduct align with Your Word and You will never forsake me.

With my whole heart I yearn for You. Don't let me wander or step aside from Your Words. May I fulfill all You have for my life.

I put Your Word in my heart, so I will not sin against You. Teach me Your Word, O Lord.

I delight myself in Your Word. Deal bountifully with me that I may live. Open my eyes that I may behold wondrous things out of Your Word.

Revive and stimulate me according to Your Word for it brings life and healing to all my flesh.

Give me understanding that I may keep Your Word with my whole heart.

Your Word causes me to walk in liberty, freedom and ease. Remember Your Word and promises to Your servant in which You have caused me to hope.

This is my comfort and consolation in my affliction; Your Word has revived me and given me life.

Teach me good judgment, wise and right discernment, and knowledge for I believe and trust in Your Word.

Let Your tender mercy and loving kindness come to me that I may live. Your Word is a lamp unto my feet and a light unto my path. I delight in Your Word.

I have hope in Your Word and I tarry for it. I pray, Lord, for Your mercy, kindness, and steadfast love to be my comfort, according to Your promises to Your servant.

Let Your mercy and loving kindness come to me that I may live, for Your Word is my delight! My life is continually in Your hands.

FAMILY

Dear Father, in the name of Jesus,

I lift up my family before You. I ask You to keep watch over them and care for them today. I pray no harm will come to them. I declare no weapon formed against them shall prosper.

I ask You to order their footsteps and may they be in the right place at the right time. I pray they will follow You and serve You all the days of their lives and that they will never depart.

Those of my family who do not know You, I ask that Your Holy Spirit will lead them and guide them to know You as Lord and Savior. Bring a Christian person into their life that they respect and look up to, someone they will listen to as they share Christ with them. Lord, Jesus, prepare their hearts to receive eternal life.

I pray for health and healing for their bodies, minds and emotions. Bless them financially and spiritually.

May they grow stronger in their walk with You every day. I forgive anything they may have said or done to me that may have hurt or wounded me in the past. I forgive and let it go that my prayers or my life will not be hindered by the enemy in any way. I give the enemy no place in my life, in Jesus' name.

Bless my family today and may we always be there for each other, always speak well of each other, and always love each other.

Thank You, Lord, for hearing this prayer in Jesus' name. Amen.

MY JABEZ PRAYER - 1 Chronicles 4:10

Father, in the name of Jesus, I ask You to bless me indeed. Bless me great, bless me big. Help me to be a success for Your Kingdom. I don't want to be average. I don't want to be an average Christian, an average minister with an average church. I don't want to be an average parent. I want to make a difference in the lives of those around me.

I don't want an average marriage with average friends. I desire to be a witness and example in everything I do. I want to be supernaturally flowing in the power of Your Holy Spirit. I want to be equipped to accomplish all You have for my life. Bless me indeed.

Enlarge my territory. Enlarge my sphere of influence. Enlarge what I have and where I am. Thank You for what You have done, but enlarge me. May every part of my life be an example of You. Everything I say, everything I do, every place I go, may I bring You Glory and be a witness to the world that You are alive and reigning in power. Break down the doors that have held me back and help me go beyond where I have never gone before. Enlarge my life.

May Your hand of power be upon me always. Open Your extended hand to me of healing, provision and open doors.

I desire Your touch upon my life. I desire Your precious touch upon me. Please, never take it from me.

Never take Your mighty hand off of me, my marriage, my family, my ministry or my church.

Keep me strong, focused, sensitive, broken, and may Your anointing be evident on my life. Keep me fresh and in tune to Your Spirit. Open Your hand of power, dear Lord.

Keep me from evil. Protect me, O Lord. Keep me from temptation, dishonor, lust of the flesh, the pride of life, greed, and offense. I pray my faith will not fail, but that I will stay strong in the power of Your Might.

Thank You, Lord, for hearing this sincere prayer. Amen.